dad's story

Keepsake Memory Journal

BY SUZANNE ZENKEL

PETER PAUPER PRESS, INC.
Rye Brook, New York

PETER PAUPER PRESS
Fine Books and Gifts Since 1928

OUR COMPANY

In 1928, at the age of twenty-two, Peter Beilenson began printing books on a small press in the basement of his parents' home in Larchmont, New York. Peter—and later, his wife, Edna—sought to create fine books that sold at "prices even a pauper could afford."

Today, still family owned and operated, Peter Pauper Press continues to honor our founders' legacy—and our customers' expectations—of beauty, quality, and value.

Designed by Heather Zschock

Copyright © 2025
Peter Pauper Press, Inc.
3 International Drive
Rye Brook, NY 10573 USA
All rights reserved
ISBN 978-1-4413-4503-5
Printed in China
7 6 5 4 3 2 1

Visit us at www.peterpauper.com

Contents

Our family tree

> Our most treasured
> heirlooms are our
> family memories.

My Great-Grandparents (YOUR GREAT-GREAT-GRANDPARENTS)

_____
NAME, BIRTH DATE & PLACE

_____
NAME, BIRTH DATE & PLACE

_____
NAME, BIRTH DATE & PLACE

_____
NAME, BIRTH DATE & PLACE

My Grandparents (YOUR GREAT-GRANDPARENTS)

_____
NAME

_____
NAME

_____
BIRTH DATE & PLACE

_____
BIRTH DATE & PLACE

My Parents (YOUR GRANDPARENTS)

_____
NAME

_____
NAME

_____
BIRTH DATE & PLACE

_____
BIRTH DATE & PLACE

Your Parents

_____
ME, YOUR DAD!

_____
NAME

_____
BIRTH DATE & PLACE

_____
BIRTH DATE & PLACE

YOU! My Child

_____
CHILD'S NAME

_____
BIRTH DATE & PLACE

To You, the Dad

Dad's Story is literally the gift of a lifetime—*your* lifetime. Once completed, it will contain information that your child will treasure. The book will tell your life story; it will answer your child's questions about his or her roots, and provide an invaluable context for his or her own life.

Divided into nine chapters, each containing clear prompts and questions, *Dad's Story* provides an easy framework into which you record your living history. Each chapter ends with a page for photos, memorabilia, and free writing.

The idea is to allow your child to know who you are—besides, of course, being their dad. It's your chance to inspire the next generation with your life experience and accomplishments.

There's also a lot of fun in learning about your day-to-day life, especially as you grew up. What movie star made your heart quicken? Did you have a favorite hobby? Who was the most significant world leader in your lifetime? Is it true that as much as things change, they stay the same? Your life provides the most fascinating history lesson your child will ever have.

Most valuable, though, is what your child will learn about you. The pages that follow will help reveal you as an evolving person, living life in full color. By providing your life with context and texture, you will give your child a better appreciation of who you really are. The links between you will emerge from the pages. At times your child will see him or herself in you; and through your lens, he or she will surely see interesting things about the world and about family. The connections are what matter most.

Feel free to skip over any questions that don't apply. And be sure to check your modesty at the door. The best memoirs are the ones that are unedited, and come straight from the heart.

Dad's birth and background

Once upon a time, in a far-off (or not so far-off) land, your story began, Dad. Chapter One is, appropriately, a place to record important facts about your heritage. Answer any questions you can about your roots, and help fill in the blanks for your child and for generations to come.

Dad's Birth and First Days

Dad, what is your birth date?

Birthplace

Birth weight and length

Home address

Full given name

Were you named after anyone? Explain.

What were you called? If you had a nickname, who came up with it and why?

Was there a welcoming celebration, religious or otherwise?

Are there any stories you were told about your birth?

Was there anything else notable about your babyhood?

Dad's Parents
(Your Child's Grandparents)

Dad, where were your parents born? Where did they grow up?

Did your parents or grandparents emigrate from another country? If so, where were they from and when did they emigrate? Where did they settle and why?

What is the meaning of your family's last names?

How would you describe your father?

_____

_____

_____

_____

_____

_____

_____

Does one special memory about your father stand out?

_____

_____

_____

_____

_____

_____

_____

When you were little, what did you like most about your father?

_____

_____

_____

_____

_____

_____

How would you describe your mother?

Does one special memory about your mother stand out?

When you were little, what did you like most about your mother?

In the early family days, what did your parents value most?

When you were a child, what did your parents do for a living?

- Father:

- Mother:

What interests or hobbies did they have?

- Father:

- Mother:

Name a characteristic you inherited from your father:

Name a characteristic you inherited from your mother:

What were your parents' religious beliefs when you were young? Did they change?

Did they have any special expressions you remember them saying often?

What was at least one important thing you learned...

- ...from your father?

- ...from your mother?

Dad's Grandparents
(Your Child's Great-Grandparents)

*What do you remember about **your** grandparents? (Where were they born? Where did they grow up? What did they do for work and enjoyment? What did you do together? What did you call them? How many children did they have?)*

- On your father's side:

- On your mother's side:

Notes

CHAPTER TWO

Dad's childhood and teenage years

Yes, "Kids are kids," as they say, but not when the kid in question is Dad! There's something utterly fascinating and absolutely transporting in picturing a dad as a real-life child. So step out of the snapshots of those family photo albums and present yourself to your child in vivid 3-D.

Dad's Childhood Years

Dad, as a child, who were you told you resembled, if anyone?

Home address:

What do you remember about your home?

What do you remember about your room?

What language or languages were spoken in your home?

Did you have a best friend? Describe.

Who were your other close friends?

Favorite hobbies or activities as a child:

Did you prefer playing inside or outside . . . or both?

Favorite games:

Favorite toy or special object:

Did you take music or any other lessons?

Did you get an allowance? If so, how much?

What did you spend it on?

What was your family car like?

Did you collect anything?

Favorite foods:

Favorite home-cooked food:

Was there anything you hated to eat?

Favorite ice cream flavor:

What was your favorite holiday and why?

What was the most memorable gift you received?

Favorite books:

Favorite radio or TV shows:

Favorite movies:

Favorite TV or movie star:

Favorite singer or group:

Did you regularly listen or watch with anyone? With whom?

Favorite spectator sport:

Favorite athlete:

What was the most memorable event you attended?

Favorite color:

What were some of the silly (or naughty) things you remember doing?

What scared you?

How did your parents discipline you if you did something wrong?

What were your chores or responsibilities?

What did you want to be when you grew up?

Dad's Siblings

Dad, list your siblings, in order of their births:

What recollections about them stand out? What did you do for fun together?

Were there relatives with whom you and your siblings were particularly close? Which ones? And what made them special to you? Where did they live?

Dad's Teenage Years

Dad, when you were a teenager, who were your close friends?

Who or what were your top:
- Musical groups/singers? How did you listen to them (LPs, cassettes, radio, live concerts, etc.)?

- Books?

- Magazines?

- Radio or TV programs?

- Movies?

- Movie stars?

- Dances?

- Sports teams?

- Athletes?

- Food or foods?

Did you play a sport or sports?

What were some of the fads or fashions?

How was your hair styled?

Did you mostly follow the styles of the day, or did you blaze your own trail?

Did you have a favorite item of clothing that you wore a lot?

What stores did you shop in? Whom did you shop with?

Who did you dream of being (or looking) like?

Did you have any idols/heroes?

What was the approximate cost of:

- A candy bar?
- A movie ticket?
- A postage stamp?
- A phone call?

What were some expressions teens frequently used?

Did you live in the same house throughout your teen years? If not, how many times did you move, and from where to where?

Did you have a favorite room in your house or place where you met friends?

As a teen, how did you get along with your parents?

• Father:

• Mother:

Did you work? If so, what did you do? How much did you earn?

Were you involved in any causes, political or otherwise?

Did you learn to drive? If so, who taught you? What car did you use?

As a Child and a Teen

Did you have any pets? If so, what kind, and what were their names?

Did you have a favorite pet? Describe.

Where did you go on family vacations or holidays?

Do you have any special vacation recollections?

How were your summers spent?

Did you have any special family traditions, including holidays or other occasions? With whom were they spent?

What were your family's everyday rituals (e.g., bedtime reading; dinnertime; listening to the radio or watching TV; playing games; prayer)?

As a young person, would you say you were (circle one and explain):

• Quiet

• Chatty

• Somewhere in between

Describe your personality.

Were there hardships to overcome as a youngster? If so, how did you do it?

What modern conveniences or technologies were not part of your early years?

What one word might people have used to describe you as a child or teen?

Why?

PHOTOS • MEMORIES • MEMORABILIA • MUSINGS

Notes

CHAPTER THREE

Dad's student life

This chapter provides a chance for you to write the book on your education, letting your child see just how you got to know so much! Whether you feel you owe it all to your alma mater, to life experience, or both, your child will surely learn a thing or two from your candid thoughts on this important subject.

Dad's Primary or Elementary Education

What primary schools did you attend and where were they located?

When were you a student there?

Did you have any favorite teachers? If so, what made them special?

What were your favorite subjects and activities?

Did anything give you particular difficulty?

Were you in any school concerts or plays?

Did you play any sports?

What did you do after school?

Do you have any especially fond recollections of your early school experience?

If you attended religious school, where was it, and what did you study?

Dad's Secondary Education

What school or schools did you attend, and where were they located?

What years did you attend?

What were your favorite subjects?

What subjects came the most easily to you?

What subjects gave you the most difficulty?

Did you have any memorable teachers? If so, what made them special?

Were you involved in any activities or sports?

Were you a member of any school clubs?

What was your social life like?

What was the most useful thing you learned?

What were the highlights of your school years?

How would you describe your overall secondary school experience?

Dad's Further Education

What high school did you attend, and where was it located?

What years did you attend?

What were your favorite subjects?

What subjects came the most easily to you?

What subjects gave you the most difficulty?

Did you have any favorite or memorable teachers? If so, what made them special?

Were you involved in extracurricular activities or sports?

Did you ever get involved in horseplay or hijinks?

Were you a member of any school clubs?

What was your social life like?

What was the most important or useful thing you learned in high school?

What was the least useful thing you learned in high school?

What were the highlights of your high school years?

What were your goals after high school?

Generally, do you remember your high school experience as being fun or difficult, or a combination of the two?

Dad's Post-Graduation Years

Did you go to college, trade school, or the military? If so, where and when?

What did you study, or for which branch did you serve? What was your focus?

Did you live at home or away? Describe your living situation.

Who were your close friends?

Were you a member of a fraternity or other social club?

Did you earn a degree (or honors) or ascend to a rank? If so, in what?

What were the highlights of your post-graduation experience?

Did you pursue any other education or training?

Do you have any regrets about your experiences?

Do you have any general thoughts about education, training, or military service that may be helpful to future generations?

Notes

CHAPTER FOUR

Dad's love and marriage

*Your kids would love to know more
about their parents and how it all began.
After all, your relationship generated a whole
new branch of the family tree. Please provide
as many details as you can.*

How, where, and when did you meet your spouse?

How old were you?

What did you find most appealing about your future spouse?

How long did you date before you decided to get married?

Did you get formally engaged? If so, where and when?

Was there a wedding shower? If so, who hosted it and where was it held?

Where and when did you get married? What was the wedding like?

What did you wear?

Who were some members of your wedding party?

Did you go on a honeymoon? If so, where, and for how long?

Do you have any honeymoon stories, funny or otherwise, to share?

Is (or was) yours a marriage of many years? If so, to what do you attribute your long-lasting relationship? (If not, why do you think it did not last?)

Where was your first home together?

When did you first meet your spouse's family and what were your impressions of them?

What were your favorite things to do together as a couple?

Who have been your special friends as a couple through the years?

Did you get married more than once? If so, to whom?

Any stories to share about your marriage or adventures with your spouse?

CHAPTER FIVE

Dad's parenthood and family life

*Here's where you took that momentous
first step on the way to parenting! These years
were undoubtedly jam-packed with activity, calling upon
total love, patience, energy, empathy, dedication, and the
most extraordinary juggling skills imaginable.*

Please list full names and birth dates of your child or children.

Was there anything notable about the birth(s)?

Did you name your child(ren) after anyone?

If there are godparents, who are they?

Where did you raise your family? What was your home like?

Did you keep baby books?

Can you share a story about your child(ren) or any childhood antics?

What were some of the special things you did as a family?

How were summers and vacations spent?

Were there any trips you remember most vividly?

Were there favorite meals or dishes you prepared? Share some recipes here.

Favorite Recipes:

Ingredients: Directions:

Favorite Recipes:

Ingredients: Directions:

Were there any special friends your family spent a lot of time with?

Did religion play a big role in your family's life?

What were the most important values you tried to instill in your child(ren)?

What was the best part of raising a family?

What was the trickiest part of raising a family?

Do you have any words of wisdom or advice on parenting?

CHAPTER SIX

Dad's work and community

*What you choose to do with your time says
a lot about you. Whether you raised your
children full time, worked outside the home,
or both, your contributions to your household
and community have been invaluable—
and a big part of your life story.*

What was your very first job? How old were you? Describe.

Are you employed? Retired?

What is (or was) your occupation?

For whom and where have you worked?

Have you had any special mentors?

What was your best job, so far, and why?

What was your worst job, so far, and why?

Do you have any ideas or tips about choosing a career?

What business or investment advice can you offer that you may have learned from your successes and/or failures?

Have you been involved in community organizations or causes? If so, what kind of work have you done? At what times in your life?

Notes

CHAPTER SEVEN

Dad's religion and spirituality

How do you nurture your soul?
This chapter will let you share with your
child your beliefs about religion
and spirituality, and the role they've
played in your life to date.

Do you have a religious affiliation?

How do you practice your religion or spirituality?

Is religion or spirituality a driving force in your life?

Are you a member of any congregation or religious organization?

Do you have a favorite prayer or sacred passage?

Did you say a special bedtime prayer as a child? If so, what was it?

Did you say a special bedtime prayer with your own child or children?

Do you say a prayer before meals?

Do you have a favorite piece of sacred music?

What religious rituals or traditions are most important to you?

Did your religious or spiritual beliefs change or evolve at any point in your life? How, and what prompted the change?

Has religion or spirituality helped you get through hard times? If so, describe.

What was your most memorable religious or spiritual experience?

What kind of religious or spiritual training did you give your children?

Notes

CHAPTER EIGHT

Dad's outlook on life and living

The odds and ends of everyday life—like the objects on your night table right now—can offer the truest picture of the real you. This chapter is all about the world according to Dad. Your responses to the questions that follow will help reveal what makes up who you really are. Think fast and simply jot down the answers that come to mind.

A Glimpse Inside

Dad, how old are you now?

What do you do for fun?

What or who makes you laugh?

List three or more things a perfect day would entail.

Of what personal achievements are you most proud?

What was the hardest thing you've had to overcome, and how did you do it?

What is the best way to deal with a bully or difficult person?

Who are your best and/or oldest friends?

What's the most important thing you can do to nurture a lasting friendship?

Where have you traveled that's been most memorable? Describe.

Have you enjoyed collecting anything? Explain.

What have been the biggest cultural or fashion trends in your lifetime?

What's the oddest thing you've ever seen or heard in your life?

What's the most significant breakthrough, discovery, or invention you've witnessed (technological, medical, or other)?

What invention has directly affected or enhanced your life the most?

Who was the first national leader you voted for?

What are the most pivotal world events that happened in your lifetime?

What is your most vivid historical recollection?

Is there a cause or issue that is, or has been, particularly important to you?

What's the most adventurous thing you've done, so far?

What's the most exciting encounter you've had with a noteworthy person?

Do you speak more than one language? If so, which one(s)?

What skills or talents have you tried to develop?

Have you recently attended any lectures, courses, or workshops?

How do you make a tough decision?

How do you overcome a fear?

What advice do people seek from you?

What book are you reading now, if any?

What is on your night table or desk as you are writing this?

What would be on the menu of your perfect meal?

What are your favorite kinds of stores? Are you a bargain hunter?

If you had a motto, what would it be?

Your theme song would be:

What would your friends say is "so *you*"?

Can you share something that your child might not know about you?

Dad's Wit and Wisdom

Fill in the blanks

I believe in .... in moderation.

I believe in .... in abundance.

I don't believe in:

....

....

Something I wish I'd done more of:

....

....

....

Something I wish I'd done less of:

....

....

....

Something I still wish to do:

....

....

....

One food I cannot stand:

....

....

....

Check one:

I like to drink: coffee   tea   neither   both   other:

I am a: morning person   night owl

It's not easy being:

It's great to be:

The place where I get my best ideas:

Always have a   on hand.

You can never have enough:

People make too big a deal about:

People don't make a big enough deal about:

In my life, everyone thought I shouldn't .... ,

but I'm so glad I did, because ....

....

....

Something I admire most in others: ....

....

....

Something I admire most in myself: ....

....

....

Something I really used to dislike, but now I like: ....

....

....

....

The best thing about being my age: ....

....

....

....

My most featured role in life has been as a: ....

....

....

....

Dad's Favorite Things

Who or what are your top picks, and why?

Actors:

Writers:

Books (or type of book):

Magazines (or type of magazine) or newspapers:

Websites:

Musicians, singers, or bands (or type of music):

Artists or works of art:

Journalists or news anchors:

Movies (or type of movie):

TV shows:

Radio shows:

Kinds of shows (opera, ballet, movie, play, musical):

Public figures:

Comedians:

Spectator sports:

Athletes:

Sports to play:

Games to play:

Charities, organizations, or causes:

Day of the week:

Season:

Time of day:

Special occasion (describe):

Meal (describe):

Comfort foods:

Pick-me-ups:

Desserts:

Ice cream flavor (has it stayed the same since childhood?):

Drinks:

Outfits or designers:

Color (has it stayed the same since childhood?):

Expressions or words:

Way to communicate (by phone, writing, email, social media, or in person):

Machines or gadgets:

Extravagance:

Restaurants:

Hotels:

Place in the world:

Rainy day activity:

Sunny day activity:

Animals:

Decade or age:

Notes

CHAPTER NINE

Fatherhood

When the stork arrived, he brought the most special of deliveries! It's difficult to put into words the loving bond between a father and child. Your child cherishes having you as a guardian angel, whose love is boundless and unconditional.

Here's where you write directly to him or her, rounding out your life story in the most meaningful and personal of ways.

My thoughts and feelings when I heard you were on the way:

What I remember most about your arrival:

What it was like to meet you for the first time:

What I gave you when you were born:

What you were like as a baby:

Pet name I have for you, and how it came to be:

Special name you have for me, and how it came to be:

A story I remember from your earliest years:

Similarities between you and me:

Things you seem to have inherited from other family members:

Something you may have inherited from me:

Some special qualities I see in you:

Some of our favorite activities we do together:

A favorite memory of us:

Things you do that make me smile or laugh:

Things you do that make me proud:

A list of things to do and places to go with you:

My hopes and dreams for your future:

Dear Child,

Love,

Notes